RUN! RUN! THERE'S A GUN!

A Rhyming Book About Gun Safety for Children

RUN! RUN! THERE'S A GUN!

A Rhyming Book About Gun Safety for Children

KY'NEIKE KING

This book is dedicated to all the children impacted by gun violence in their homes, schools, and communities—your safety, well-being, and life matters.

If you're ever in a situation
where there is a gun, you should
say to yourself and others,
"Run! Run! There's a gun!"

Run! Run!
There's a gun!

Never touch a gun or point it at others.
It is very dangerous, protect
your friends just like you would
your sisters and brothers.

If you see a gun at school even if it is brought there by someone you know, you should find an adult to tell and show.

If someone begins shooting
a gun where you are at, find a place
to run and hide- STAT!

Never move a gun. Leave it where it was found. Alert an adult and stop other children from coming around.

A bad guy with a gun could be
in any of the places you go,
so what you'll do during a shooting
is something you should know.

Hide in a dark place, and don't speak a word, until you are sure it's a police officer's voice you've heard.

Some good people carry guns too;
some may even be related to you.
There are police officers, you will
recognize their uniforms in the color blue.
Their job is to serve and protect you.

A bad guy with a gun could be someone
you know or someone you don't;
either way, changing how you respond,
you won't!

Detectives, security guards,
and some business owners have guns.
They use them to protect themselves
and others from the "bad" ones.

Guns are used for training, by hunters, and by our military men and women. But, the opportunity for them to get in the wrong hands should not be given.

Although not everyone with a gun is a bad guy, this is true. When in an uncomfortable situation with a gun, it's still important you know what to do:

● Don't touch the gun or allow any friends to. Keeping your distance is the safest thing for you.

● Immediately tell someone you trust, remember gun safety starts with all of us.

● If you see or hear someone shooting a gun, run to a safe place as fast as you can. Hiding from the shooter is the best plan.

● It's up to all of us to do our part to keep each other safe, prepared, and smart.

● Keep your eyes open and your ears sharp, reading about what to do is just the start. What to do to keep yourself safe, and others too, Is important! We are depending on you.

If you're ever in a situation
where there is a gun and you feel unsafe,
you should quickly go to a different place.
Get the attention of someone you trust
and tell them about the gun-You must!

MY SAFE PLACE

List **5** things that make you feel safe:

1

2

3

4

5

PRACTICE THESE STEPS FOR INCREASED GUN SAFETY

Do not go near a gun. Stay away.

Once you see a gun, assume it's loaded.

Never touch a gun. You should not touch, hold or pick-up a gun.

Tell an adult or authority figure if you see a gun or know that someone has a gun. Immediately leave the area where the gun is to reduce the chances of injury.

NOTE TO PARENTS

Secure guns in a lockbox or use a gun lock and keep it in a safe place.

Always keep guns out of the hands of children and untrained persons.

Firearms are for the persons who purchased them legally. Report lost or stolen guns and other firearms.

Every gun or firearm in the residence should be registered.Every parent has a role in keeping their child safe from the dangers of guns and other firearms in the home.

MATCH THE WORDS WITH THEIR DEFINITIONS ACTIVITY

ACCESSING ●

ALERT ●

STAT ●

UNSAFE ●

UNCOMFORTABLE ●

a) *Instantly or immediately*

b) *Not safe/Dangerous*

c) *Quick to notice any unusual and potentially dangerous or difficult circumstance*

d) *Causing or feeling slight pain or physical discomfort*

e) *A means of approaching or entering a place*

COLORING PAGE

So, remember, if you're ever in a situation where there is a gun, you should say to yourself and others, "Run! Run! There's a gun!"

YOUTH GUN SAFETY LEADER
AWARDED TO:

____

For learning, practicing and sharing
how to be safe around guns and other firearms.